First published in 2025 by Allsorted Ltd, WD19 4BG U.K.

The authorised representative in the EU is
Petit Pop Agencies, Unit 8 Robinhood Business Park, Robinhood Road,
Dublin 22, D22 A370, Ireland (email: info@petitpop.com)

The facts and statistics in this book are correct up to the end of 2024. Data comes from publicly available sources and is presented as correct as far as our knowledge allows. Any views or opinions represented in this book are personal and belong solely to the book author and are not intended to malign any religious community, ethnic group, club, organisation, company or individual.

ISBN 9781917535144

EPIC
ADVENTURE
CLUB

How to

Fight a Dinosaur

(and win!)

ALLSORTED.
WD19 4BG U.K.

CONTENTS

How to fight a...
TYRANNOSAURUS REX

KILLER FACT

The T. rex can gulp down small dinosaurs whole – NO CHEWING NEEDED!

STATS

HEIGHT	6 M
WEIGHT	7000 KG
LENGTH	12 M
KILLER RATING	10/10
INTELLIGENCE	3/10

STRENGTH
The Mighty Bite

Watch out for the T. rex's super-strong bite. Its teeth are like giant, sharp bananas that can crush anything. The T. rex also has a sense of smell so strong it can sniff you out from afar – so have a bath before you think about coming out of hiding.

WEAKNESS
Not So Nimble

The T. rex is not very quick on its feet and it can't turn around fast.

Its top speed is 20 km/h, about half as quick as a sprinting human. So if you move like a ninja, you can stay out of its way.

TIPS AND TACTICS
Use Your Surroundings

Trees, rocks and even big puddles can be your best friends when a T. rex is nearby! These natural obstacles can block its vision or slow it down, giving you precious moments to think. Use a tree to climb high and stay out of reach, or duck behind a massive rock to stay hidden. Even puddles or muddy patches can help if the T. rex slips or gets slowed down.

How to fight a...
VELOCIRAPTOR

KILLER FACT

They have deadly sharp claws and use them to slash at prey with incredible precision.

STATS

HEIGHT	0.5 M
WEIGHT	14 KG
LENGTH	1.8 M
KILLER RATING	8/10
INTELLIGENCE	8/10

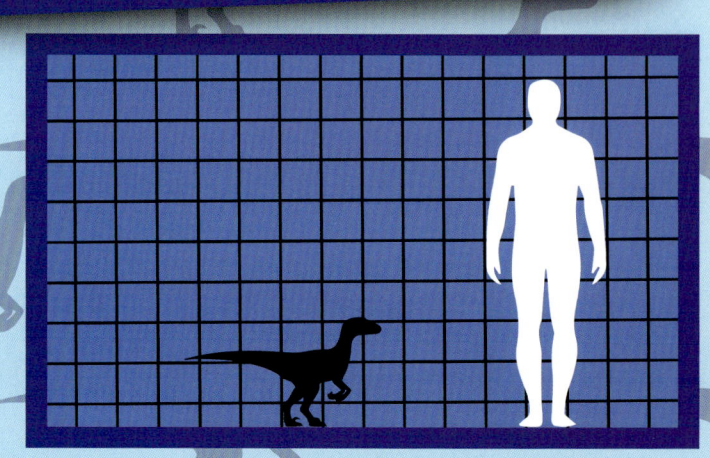

STRENGTH
Speedy Hunter

The Velociraptor is fast, clever and deadly. It runs up to 40 km/h and uses its sharp, curved claws to grab prey. Velociraptors are smart too, hunting in groups to catch their prey. With speed, sharp claws and teamwork, they are fierce predators.

WEAKNESS
Small Size

It is small, only about the size of a turkey, which makes it vulnerable to larger predators.

Its lightweight body means it isn't very strong and Velociraptors aren't great climbers either.

TIPS AND TACTICS
One Step Ahead

Climbing to higher ground can keep you safe. If one gets too close, grab a sturdy stick or rock to protect yourself.

Since Velociraptors rely on teamwork, staying away from groups can hinder them and give you an advantage. Always stay alert – they're sneaky and love to catch their prey by surprise.

How to fight a...
TYRANNOTITAN

KILLER FACT

Its jaws pack a bone-crushing bite, delivering more force than even modern-day alligators!

STATS

HEIGHT	4 M
WEIGHT	7000 KG
LENGTH	12 M
KILLER RATING	9/10
INTELLIGENCE	4/10

STRENGTH
Raw Power

The Tyrannotitan's strength comes from its colossal size, powerful jaws and muscular build. With the ability to deliver crushing blows with its legs and tail, it overpowers most predators through sheer force and aggression.

WEAKNESS
Speed Trap

The Tyrannotitan's massive size likely limits its speed, making it much slower than smaller, more agile predators like the Velociraptor.

TIPS AND TACTICS
Unleash Your Power

Create a Tyrannotitan tail using a long, sturdy rope or foam pool noodle. Attach it to a belt around your waist and practise swinging it like a massive weapon. For leg strikes, practise powerful kicks, imagining you're using your massive legs to deliver a crushing blow. Pair up with a friend and practise using your "tail" to knock over obstacles or block incoming "attacks", simulating the power of a Tyrannotitan in combat.

How to fight a...
TRICERATOPS

KILLER FACT

The Triceratops uses its horns to knock down ANYTHING in its path!

STATS

HEIGHT   3 M
WEIGHT   6000 KG
LENGTH   9 M
KILLER RATING   8/10
INTELLIGENCE   6/10

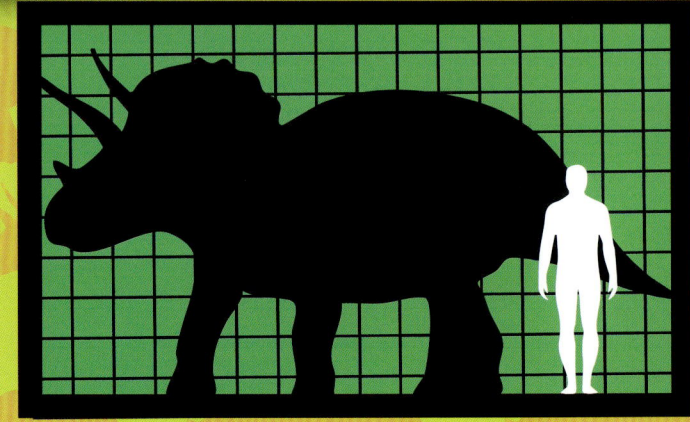

STRENGTH
Horns of Power

The Triceratops is a powerhouse with its bony frill and three sharp horns. Its frill acts like a shield, and its horns fend off any predator. Strong and sturdy, the Triceratops stands tall to protect itself and its herd from danger.

WEAKNESS
Limited Energy

The Triceratops lacks stamina. While it's strong and capable of defending itself with its horns, it's not built for long, drawn-out fights. If a predator can wear it down with quick, strategic moves, the Triceratops might tire.

TIPS AND TACTICS
Stamina Success

Stay out of range of its sharp horns, which can easily injure you, and use your stamina to your advantage.

Try to confuse it or distract it from its herd, where it feels safest, and wear it out. Remember, the Triceratops is more dangerous when it feels threatened, so keep your distance and wait for an opening!

How to fight a...
BRACHIOSAURUS

KILLER FACT

Its heart is the size of a large dustbin, pumping blood all the way up its long neck to its head!

STATS

HEIGHT	12 M
WEIGHT	50000 KG
LENGTH	25 M
KILLER RATING	3/10
INTELLIGENCE	4/10

STRENGTH
A Towering Giant

The Brachiosaurus is one of the largest dinosaurs ever to walk the Earth. Its size gives it huge strength, and it's also incredibly sturdy, able to withstand attacks with its thick, heavy body. Trying to take it down is impossible without a serious strategy.

WEAKNESS
The Underbelly

With its long neck and heavy body, the Brachiosaurus struggles to change direction quickly or defend itself from attackers. Its towering height makes it an easy target for predators aiming for its legs or underbelly, which is less protected.

TIPS AND TACTICS
Quick Feet

Focus on its massive torso and tree-trunk legs. Its height makes it hard for it to defend its lower body and a well-placed strike to the legs can bring it down.

Stay out of range of its long neck, as it can swing it around to knock you away. Since the Brachiosaurus is slow to turn, use that to your advantage by staying quick on your feet and attacking from unexpected angles!

How to fight a...
TORVOSAURUS

KILLER FACT

It has jaws so powerful they can crush the bones of even the biggest prey!

STATS

HEIGHT	3.5 M
WEIGHT	4500 KG
LENGTH	9 M
KILLER RATING	9/10
INTELLIGENCE	3/10

STRENGTH
Mighty Tail Swings

With big, powerful legs and teeth like sharp knives, this giant dinosaur is built to chase and catch its lunch – and it can knock down bigger dinosaurs with one swipe of its tail! It uses its muscle and power to get what it wants.

WEAKNESS
Line of Vision

The Torvosaurus has forward-facing eyes for depth perception, but this could mean it has blind spots to the sides or behind it. Its sheer size means it needs a massive territorial range to find enough food and so it has to spend a lot of time patrolling to protect it.

TIPS AND TACTICS
Side Attack

Staying low and out of its direct line of sight could be an advantage.

Find cover and attack the sides of the Torvosaurus, where it can't see you. Use its big size against it by making quick moves it can't match. Then, if you can, aim for its eyes – it is a sensitive spot!

How to fight a...
DILOPHOSAURUS

KILLER FACT

It hunts with blistering speed, and a bone-chilling roar!

STATS

HEIGHT	1.8 M
WEIGHT	400 KG
LENGTH	7 M
KILLER RATING	8/10
INTELLIGENCE	1/10

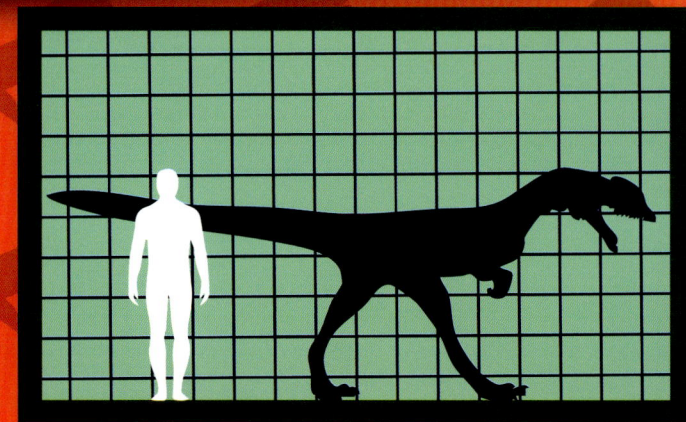

STRENGTH
Small But Mighty

The Dilophosaurus might not be the biggest dino around, but it's still a ferocious beast. It's got sharp teeth and a strong jaw, perfect for biting into its prey. With its powerful legs, it can run fast to chase down food, and it's got a tail that can help it balance while it moves.

WEAKNESS
Tiny Arms

Its body is light and not as strong as some of the bigger predators, so it could get knocked over easily in a fight. Also, its arms are pretty small for a dinosaur, which means it can't grab or hold onto things very well.

TIPS AND TACTICS
Watch Out for the Teeth!

Keep your distance from its head, as this dinosaur's sharp teeth are its most dangerous weapon.

Focus on using its lack of arm strength and length to your advantage. Its short arms, which are about 30–40 cm (12–16 inches) long, cannot grab or hold anything effectively, so you're safe from any grappling attempts.

How to fight an...
ALLOSAURUS

KILLER FACT

It can bite and shake its head from side to side, quickly tearing through its prey!

STATS

HEIGHT	4.5 M
WEIGHT	2000 KG
LENGTH	12 M
KILLER RATING	9/10
INTELLIGENCE	5/10

STRENGTH
Bendy-Necked Beast

It has an incredibly flexible neck. It is almost like a snake with legs, making it a master of quick strikes! Its neck can bend and twist easily, thanks to its unique bones and muscles, allowing it to snap at prey in an instant.

WEAKNESS
Not Invincible

While strong enough for quick, precise bites, this dinosaur's light skull isn't built to withstand heavy impacts or prolonged struggles. If a dinosaur like the Stegosaurus lands a powerful tail swipe to its head, it can seriously injure or even knock out the Allosaurus.

TIPS AND TACTICS
Speed and Strategy

Work on your agility and speed – staying light on your feet is crucial.

Also, sharpen your accuracy; you'll need precise aim to strike its moving head or neck. Remember, distance is your friend – stay quick, stay sharp, and don't let it close the gap!

How to fight a...
CERATOSAURUS

KILLER FACT

The unique horn on its nose may be used to impress mates or defend against rivals!

STATS

HEIGHT 2.5 M
WEIGHT 970 KG
LENGTH 6 M
KILLER RATING 8/10
INTELLIGENCE 6/10

STRENGTH
Quick and Tough

Watch out for its strong jaws and sharp teeth! This dino may be small, but it's quick and tough, with a horn on its nose that can be used for defence. Its long tail helps it balance as it moves fast and those powerful legs give it a good jump if it needs to strike.

WEAKNESS
Clumsy Predator

The Ceratosaurus loves to hang out by rivers and lakes. But on dry land, it's a lot more awkward, like someone trying to creep around in flip-flops, and it has a much harder time surprising its prey and staying safe.

TIPS AND TACTICS
Keep It Dry

The key to dealing with the Ceratosaurus is to keep it far away from water. This predator thrives in environments where it can use its ambush skills, which are significantly enhanced near lakes, rivers or swamps. The absence of water will limit its ability to conceal itself and launch surprise attacks. But always remain vigilant, as even outside its preferred habitat the Ceratosaurus remains an aggressive predator.

How to fight a...
TARBOSAURUS

KILLER FACT

The Tarbosaurus has an unusually long skull, giving it extra room for super-sharp teeth.

STATS

HEIGHT	3.5 M
WEIGHT	4500 KG
LENGTH	10 M
KILLER RATING	9/10
INTELLIGENCE	5/10

STRENGTH
Tail of Triumph

The Tarbosaurus has an incredible sense of balance. With its long, heavy tail acting like a counterweight, it's stable, even when charging or turning quickly. This balance makes it precise with its attacks, using its jaws to land a powerful bite without stumbling.

WEAKNESS
Teeth Trouble

The Tarbosaurus relies on its incredible bite force, but its teeth are better suited for crushing than slicing. Interestingly, its powerful jaws can sometimes work against it – biting down on something too hard can cause it to break its own teeth. Ouch!

TIPS AND TACTICS
Jaw Juggernaut

If you need to slow it down, toss something sturdy – like a rock or a thick log – for it to crunch on. That'll buy you a few precious seconds to make your escape. But don't get too confident – once it's done with its chew toy, you're right back on the menu!

How to fight an...
EINIOSAURUS

KILLER FACT

The Einiosaurus uses its sharp horns in battles with other herd members as a show of strength!

STATS

HEIGHT	2 M
WEIGHT	1200 KG
LENGTH	6 M
KILLER RATING	2/10
INTELLIGENCE	4/10

STRENGTH
Defensive Power

Watch out: this dino's powerful legs give it the strength to charge at you if you get too close and those sharp horns can jab you if you're not careful.

It's a tough herbivore, ready to defend itself.

WEAKNESS
Smell Sense

While it can see well, the Einiosaurus' sense of smell isn't very strong so it might not notice predators approaching from far away. This makes it easier for sneaky or quick animals to catch it off guard, especially if they use their nose to find it first.

TIPS AND TACTICS
Prepare Well

To prepare for a fight, practise your agility at home.

Set up an obstacle course with cones, cushions or chairs to improve weaving and dodging. Try to quickly change direction, as in a real battle, as this will help you avoid the Einiosaurus' powerful charge and sharp horns.

How to fight a...
STEGOSAURUS

KILLER FACT

The Stegosaurus' powerful tail can break the bones of a predator in just one blow!

STATS

HEIGHT	3.5 M
WEIGHT	5000 KG
LENGTH	9 M
KILLER RATING	2/10
INTELLIGENCE	2/10

STRENGTH
The Armoured Defender

The Stegosaurus is built for defence. With its huge, spiked tail, it can deliver a powerful blow to any predator that gets too close. The plates on its back aren't just for show – they help protect it from attacks and might even regulate its temperature.

WEAKNESS
Tiny Brain

The Stegosaurus is not very quick. Also, while its tail is powerful, it can only use it effectively if the enemy is right behind it, so it struggles with front or side attacks. And its small brain means it doesn't have the quick thinking to outsmart a clever predator.

TIPS AND TACTICS
Side Attacks

Your best bet is to avoid getting too close to its powerful tail. Use its slow pace to your advantage. Be stealthy, dashing around it to attack from the side or front, where it's less protected. You could also try fooling it by throwing stones to its side, so that it turns away from you and gets confused.

How to fight a...
SPINOSAURUS

KILLER FACT

Its powerful tail is well suited for swimming, acting like a giant paddle.

STATS

HEIGHT   5 M
WEIGHT   7400 KG
LENGTH   14 M
KILLER RATING   10/10
INTELLIGENCE   4/10

STRENGTH
Speedy Swimmer

This intimidating dino has massive jaws. It can snap through bones as if they are jelly and those long claws are perfect for slashing or grabbing its prey. The flat bones on its back are like a huge sail, and might work like a shark's fin in water.

WEAKNESS
Sail Trouble

The Spinosaurus' huge sail makes it easier for predators to spot from a distance and slows it down when it needs to hide or sneak up on prey. Its long, crocodile-like snout is perfect for catching fish but not as good for grabbing fast land animals.

TIPS AND TACTICS
Find Your Inner Cowboy

Using a lasso could be a clever tactic to manage its enormous snout. If you're quick and precise, try to loop a lasso around its jaws to limit its movements, making it harder for the creature to strike or use its powerful bite.

Use the environment to your advantage – just like a cowboy herding cattle.

33

How to fight a...
CONCAVENATOR

KILLER FACT

Its sharp claws are so powerful it can grab prey like a supercharged grappling hook!

STATS

HEIGHT	2 M
WEIGHT	400 KG
LENGTH	6 M
KILLER RATING	5/10
INTELLIGENCE	5/10

STRENGTH
Strong and Steady

Two tall bones on the Concavenator's spine make a hump a bit like a camel's, helping with temperature changes and balance. It has powerful muscles and sharp claws on its arms to grab prey. Its strong back legs help it move fast and stay balanced and steady.

WEAKNESS
Don't Get the Hump

The special hump on its back might make it harder to move quickly, the extra weight slowing it down and making dodging attacks more difficult. Plus, the hump could be an easy target, making it vulnerable during battles.

TIPS AND TACTICS
Outrunning the Beast

Use its impatience against it – dodge its initial charge and force it into tight spaces where its speed is limited. Throwing heavy objects can create distractions, but don't expect it to lose interest for long. Climbing might seem like an escape, but this predator is shockingly agile, so your best bet is to keep moving, stay unpredictable, and don't let it corner you!

How to fight a...
GIGANOTOSAURUS

KILLER FACT

With jaws strong enough to crush skulls, it's one of the Earth's most powerful predators!

STATS

HEIGHT	7 M
WEIGHT	8000 KG
LENGTH	13 M
KILLER RATING	9/10
INTELLIGENCE	6/10

STRENGTH
Giant Predator

Fighting a Giganotosaurus is like facing a living bulldozer. Its teeth are as long as rulers, perfect for tearing into big prey. It has powerful legs and sharp claws on its feet to grip and hold onto its victims, making it one of the top hunters.

WEAKNESS
Giant Appetite

The Giganotosaurus needs to eat a crazy amount of food to stay strong. Every day, it must eat 1000 kg of meat – that's more than 7000 hamburgers! That's a huge challenge, because finding that much food isn't easy. It has to travel far and wide to find its next meal.

TIPS AND TACTICS
Hunger Hero

Take advantage of its hunger. If you can draw its attention away from a potential meal, you can weaken its focus. Try to create distractions or lead it away from prey, forcing it to waste energy searching for food elsewhere.

Without a fresh meal in sight, the Giganotosaurus may become weaker and more frustrated.

How to fight a...
CAUDIPTERYX

KILLER FACT

The Caudipteryx has razor-sharp claws, ready to slash at anything that's close!

STATS

HEIGHT 0.9 M
WEIGHT 2.5 KG
LENGTH 1 M
KILLER RATING 3/10
INTELLIGENCE 5/10

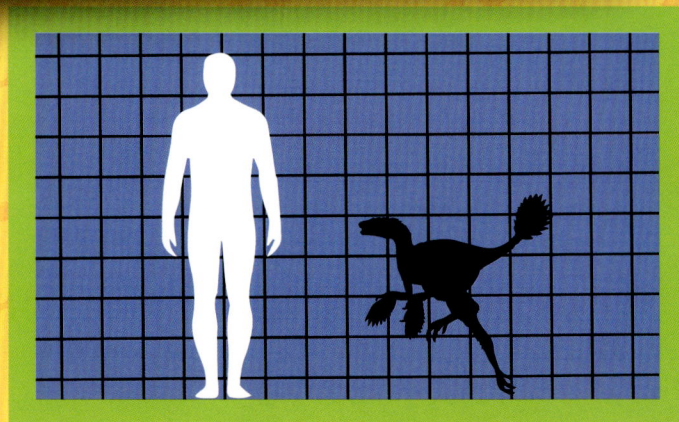

STRENGTH
Nimble Survivor

The Caudipteryx is incredibly quick, darting around to avoid danger and striking with its claws when needed. Its strong legs help it escape quickly, making it a tough opponent for any predator that underestimates it.

WEAKNESS
Small and Light

Being small and light, it isn't built for strength, so it struggles against larger, more powerful predators. Its claws, while sharp, are not designed for heavy combat and its feathered body, though useful for display, offers little protection against bigger threats.

TIPS AND TACTICS
Clear Head

Staying calm is key to making smart decisions.

Take deep breaths and focus on the situation around you. Trust your instincts and think ahead – remember, although this dinosaur is a lot smaller than others, its speed can make it very dangerous.

React with careful control, whether you're dodging attacks or planning your next move.

How to fight a...
PTERANODON

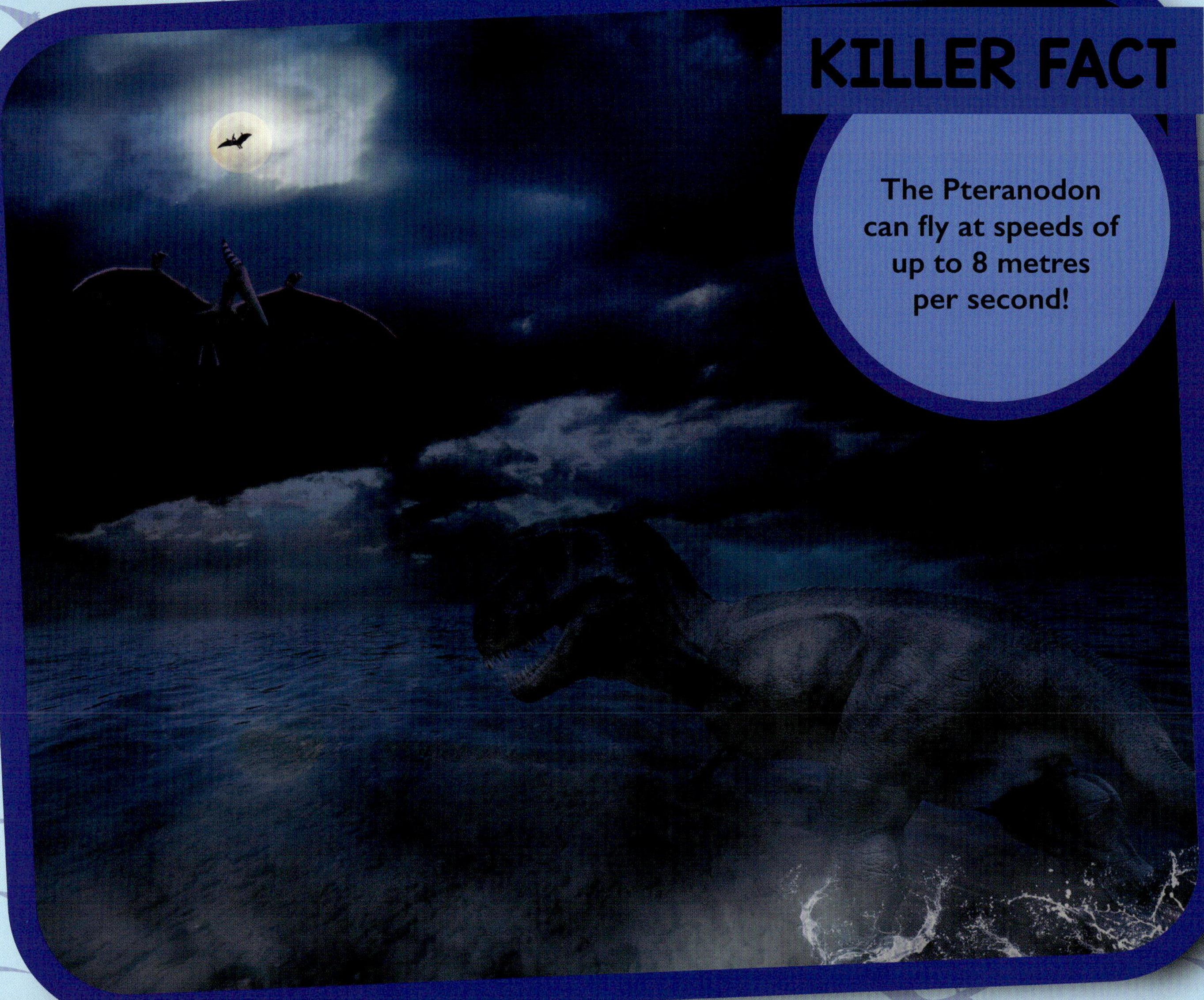

KILLER FACT

The Pteranodon can fly at speeds of up to 8 metres per second!

STATS

HEIGHT	1.8 M
WEIGHT	20 KG
WING SPAN	7 M
KILLER RATING	2/10
INTELLIGENCE	5/10

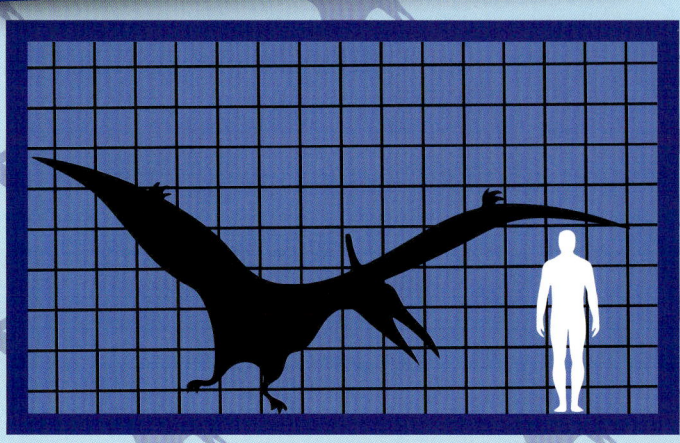

The Pteranodon is not technically a dinosaur, but it's a giant flying reptile from the Pterosaur family.

STRENGTH
The Sky's Superhero

In a fight, the Pteranodon is an expert at escaping! It's a master of flight, using its massive wings like a superhero's cape to zoom away from danger. While it might not have sharp teeth or claws, its long beak is perfect to defend itself if needed.

WEAKNESS
Soaring But Not Strong

The Pteranodon has some weaknesses. It's not built for fighting, so it struggles against larger predators, especially on the ground. Its huge wings make it hard for it to move quickly and it relies on flight to escape danger rather than physical strength.

TIPS AND TACTICS
Outwit the Sky King

Focus on its biggest weakness – its reliance on flight! First, keep it from getting a good take-off by blocking its path with obstacles. If it does take to the air, stay low and move quickly to avoid being spotted. The Pteranodon has great vision from above, so hide behind things to stay out of sight. Once it's on the ground, use your speed to close in – its massive wings slow it down, so it won't be able to escape easily!

How to fight a...
COELOPHYSIS

KILLER FACT

The Coelophysis hunts in packs, using teamwork to take down bigger prey!

STATS

HEIGHT	1 M
WEIGHT	25 KG
LENGTH	3 M
KILLER RATING	2/10
INTELLIGENCE	5/10

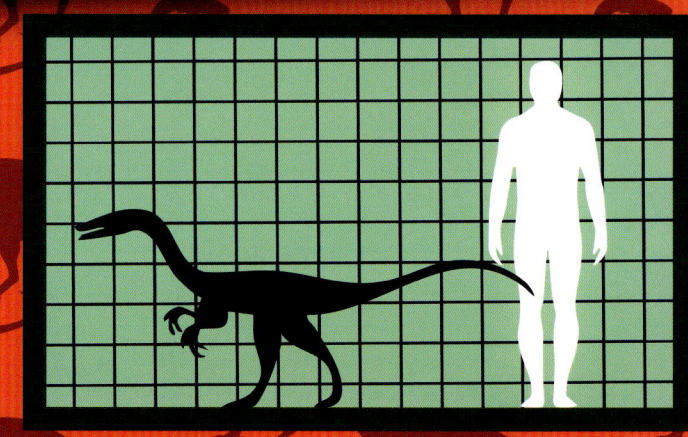

STRENGTH
Opportunistic Predator

The Coelophysis boasts a high metabolism, providing it with the stamina to hunt and remain active for extended periods. Its lightweight build enables it to navigate challenging terrain with ease. It's a skilled, opportunistic predator.

WEAKNESS
Weak Alone

While it's fast and agile, it becomes much more vulnerable if it's separated from its pack.

Alone, it lacks the strength to defend itself against larger predators and has a harder time with its foes.

TIPS AND TACTICS
The Curious Hunter

Use its curiosity against it! This small dinosaur is always on the lookout for new things, so try setting up decoys or noises that will catch its attention. While it's investigating one thing, you can sneak around and get the upper hand. The Coelophysis may be quick and agile, but it can easily be distracted by shiny objects or strange movements, making it vulnerable when it focuses on the wrong thing!

How to fight a...
STYRACOSAURUS

KILLER FACT

The Styracosaurus has up to six sharp horns on its head, making it one of the spikiest dinosaurs.

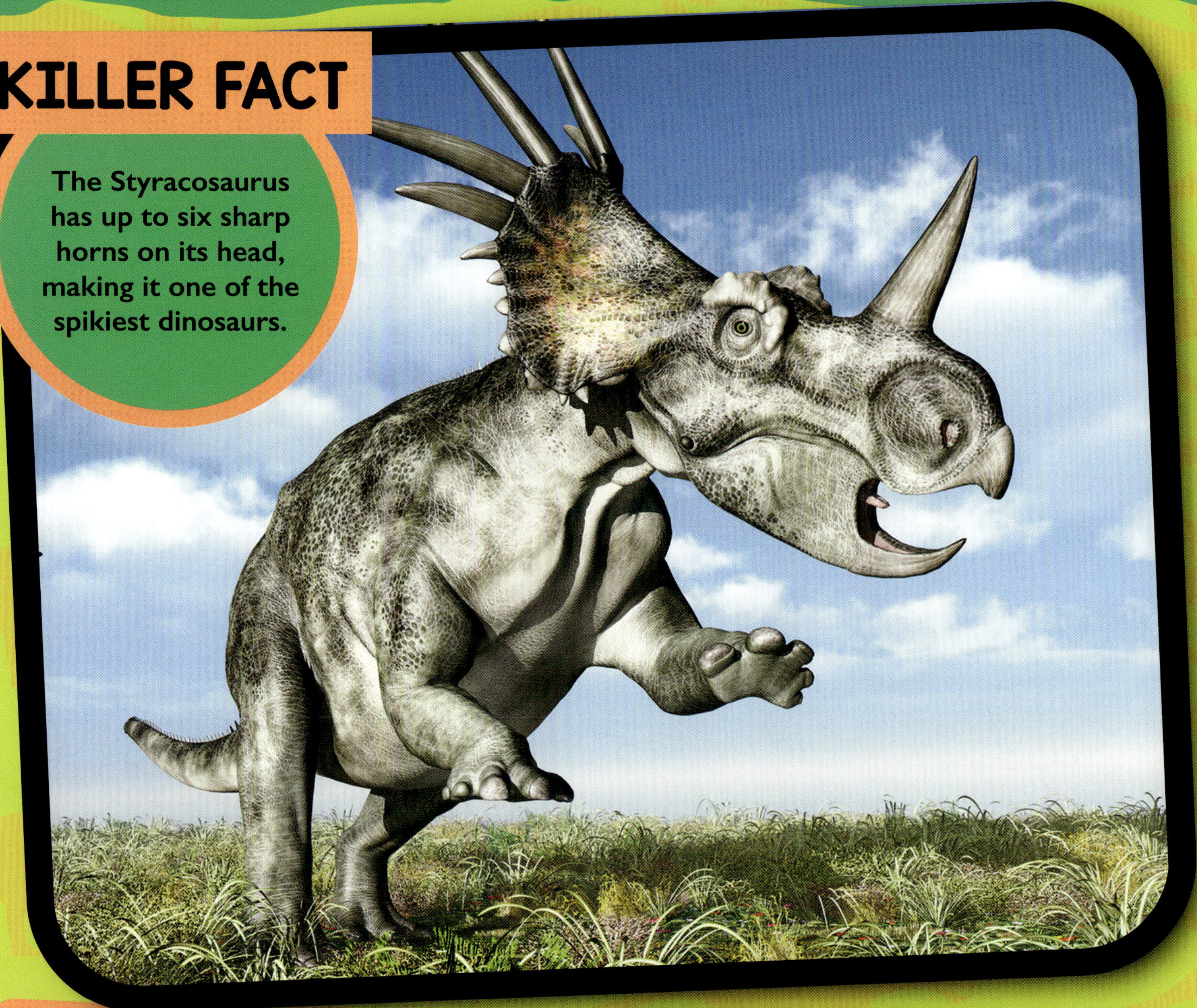

STATS

HEIGHT	2.5 M
WEIGHT	2700 KG
LENGTH	5.5 M
KILLER RATING	4/10
INTELLIGENCE	4/10

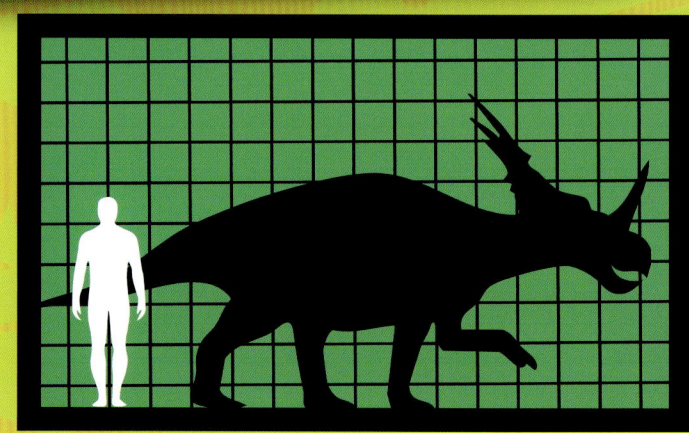

STRENGTH
Unpredictable

In a fight, the Styracosaurus surprises its enemies with its unusual defence strategy. Instead of just charging, it might turn sideways, using its long, sharp horns like a fortress to block attacks. Its large frill creates a wall of spikes that makes it nearly impossible for predators to get close.

WEAKNESS
Limited Vision

Its large frill limits its vision, making it vulnerable to surprise attacks from behind. It can't turn its heavy, spiky head very fast.

If a predator can outmanoeuvre it, the Styracosaurus might struggle to protect itself.

TIPS AND TACTICS
Dinosaur Dodge

To practise, you can play "Dinosaur Dodge" with friends! One person acts as the Styracosaurus, using its horns for defence, while the others are predators trying to sneak up from behind. The predators must use quick moves and distractions to tag the Styracosaurus without getting too close to its sharp horns. This game helps you develop agility and strategy.

How to fight a...
PARASAUROLOPHUS

KILLER FACT

A single whip of its tail can shatter a predator's ribs, making it an incredible weapon to have.

STATS

HEIGHT	4.6 M
WEIGHT	5000 KG
LENGTH	10 M
KILLER RATING	1/10
INTELLIGENCE	6/10

STRENGTH
Built-In Horn

Its most striking feature, the long, curved crest on its head, amplifies sound, creating deep, resonant calls that can travel for miles. These calls warn the herd of danger or help lost members find their way back – communication is one of its greatest strengths.

WEAKNESS
No Armour, No Claws

The Parasaurolophus has no sharp claws or teeth for defence, making it vulnerable in a direct fight. Its large crest could also make it an easy target for predators. If separated from its herd, it relies on running to escape danger.

TIPS AND TACTICS
Alarm Crest

Focus on staying calm and patient – it's not an aggressive dinosaur, but it's very alert. Try sneaking downwind so it can't catch your scent, and move quietly to avoid triggering its alarm crest. If it spots you, it's likely to run, so be ready to track it carefully. Remember, this dino's strength is in its speed and communication, so careful, silent strategy is the best way to outsmart it!

How to fight a...
DIPLODOCUS

KILLER FACT

The Diplodocus weighs more than two adult elephants!

STATS

HEIGHT	4.6 M
WEIGHT	15000 KG
LENGTH	26 M
KILLER RATING	2/10
INTELLIGENCE	4/10

STRENGTH
Tail Whip

The Diplodocus isn't a fighter, but it's still tough!

At 26 metres long (that's roughly three school buses in a row!) it's hard for predators to bring down. If needed, it swings its powerful tail like a whip, sending any attacker flying.

WEAKNESS
The Peaceful Giant

While it's huge and can defend itself with its powerful tail, it's not built for speed or fighting. Plus, since it's a plant-eater, it doesn't have sharp teeth or claws to attack with, relying mostly on its size and tail for defence.

TIPS AND TACTICS
Long Neck Advantage

A clever trick to fight a Diplodocus – though it would never want to – could be to use its own size against it. You could try distracting it with a loud noise or movement far away. While it focuses on that, you could sneak in close, staying out of reach of its powerful tail. The trick is to use its slow reaction time to your advantage, but remember, the Diplodocus is more about peace than battle!

How to fight an...
IGUANODON

KILLER FACT

Its thumb spikes are so sharp and strong they could pierce through the thick skin of a predator!

STATS

HEIGHT	4.6 M
WEIGHT	4000 KG
LENGTH	10 M
KILLER RATING	3/10
INTELLIGENCE	7/10

STRENGTH
Thumb Power

In a fight, the Iguanodon uses its powerful thumb spikes to jab at predators trying to attack, making them think twice before getting too close. Its strong legs are perfect for kicking and it can swing its long tail to push enemies back.

WEAKNESS
Slow to Escape

The Iguanodon's biggest weakness is its size and it can't escape quickly if cornered. It's especially vulnerable to predators that attack in packs. If separated from its herd, the Iguanodon becomes an easy target for faster or more aggressive hunters.

TIPS AND TACTICS
Know Your Strengths

The Iguanodon knows its sharp thumb spikes are one of its greatest strengths. They give it confidence and an edge when facing danger. Think about your own key strengths – whether it's being quick on your feet, staying calm under pressure, or using your unique skills. By understanding and using your strengths, you can handle any challenge that comes your way.

How to fight a...
MEGALOSAURUS

KILLER FACT

Its forward-facing eyes help it see in 3D and judge how far away things are.

STATS

HEIGHT	3 M
WEIGHT	1000 KG
LENGTH	9 M
KILLER RATING	7/10
INTELLIGENCE	6/10

STRENGTH
Impressive Hunter

Using its keen eyesight, the Megalosaurus quietly stalks its target, blending into the environment. Once close, it launches a swift attack using its powerful legs. This method of ambush is especially effective for hunting in dense vegetation and low-light conditions.

WEAKNESS
Low Stamina

While it excels in short bursts of speed for ambushing prey, it may struggle in extended battles. If faced with an opponent that can outlast it or wear it down over time, the Megalosaurus could tire quickly, losing its effectiveness in the fight and leaving it vulnerable.

TIPS AND TACTICS
Clever Tricks

This dinosaur might not expect strange noises or sudden movements. You could create a distraction, making loud rustling noises in shrubbery around it to draw its attention. Use its reliance on sight and stay hidden in shadows or behind rocks. A Megalosaurus may be strong, but it can be fooled by clever tricks – just make sure to stay out of reach when it comes charging back!

How to fight a...
KENTROSAURUS

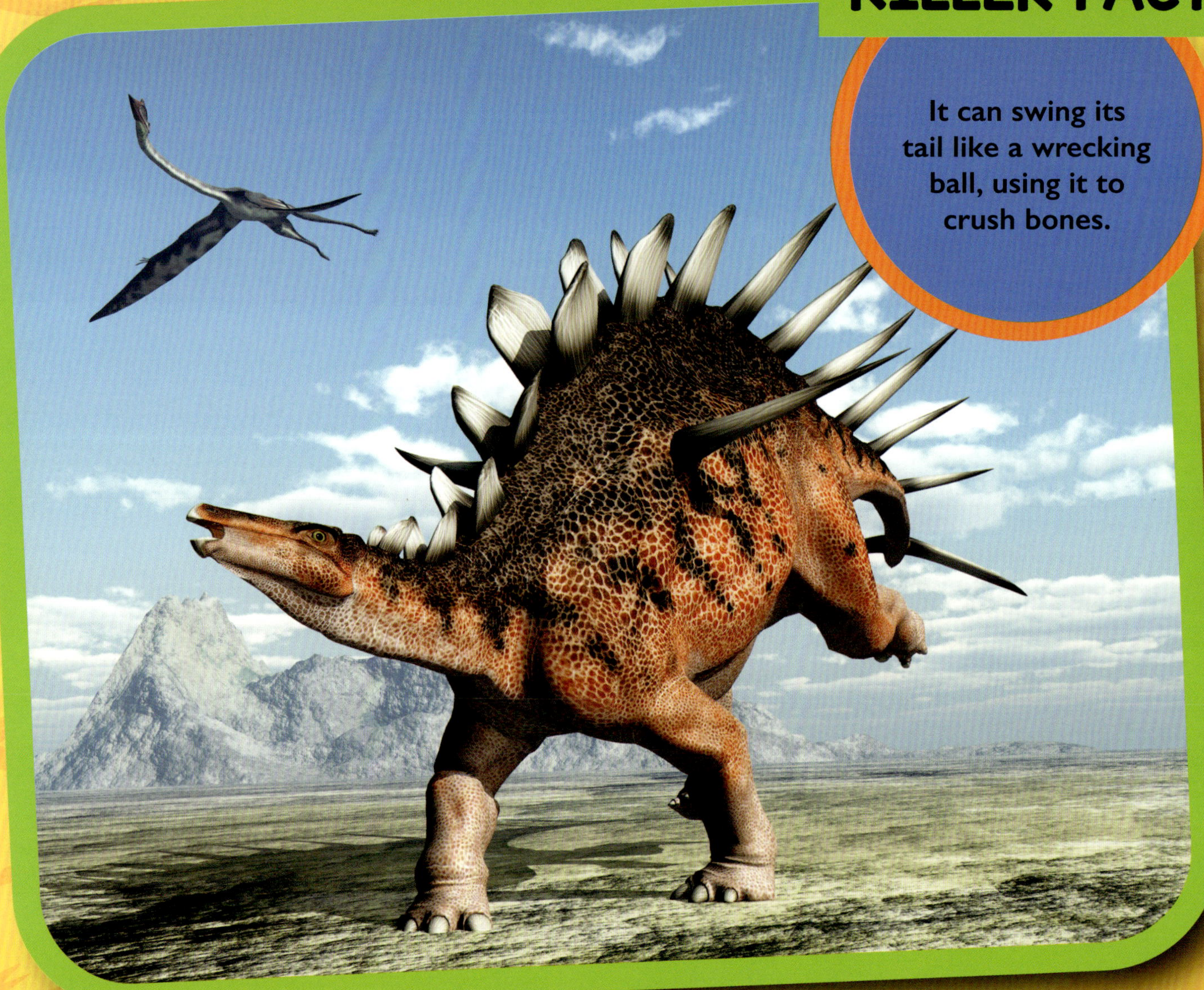

KILLER FACT

It can swing its tail like a wrecking ball, using it to crush bones.

STATS

HEIGHT	1.8 M
WEIGHT	1600 KG
LENGTH	5 M
KILLER RATING	6/10
INTELLIGENCE	2/10

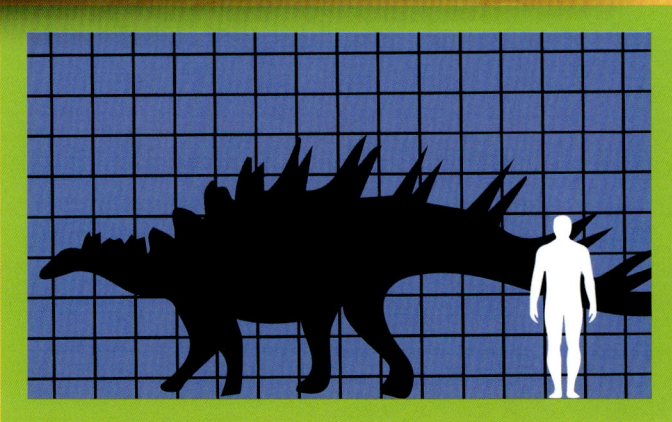

STRENGTH
Walking Fortress

The Kentrosaurus is armed with sharp spikes along its back and a powerful tail. With enough force to pierce thick skin or shatter bones, this tail makes it a fearsome opponent, proving that even plant-eaters can pack a punch in the fight for survival.

WEAKNESS
Small Size

Its small size compared to larger predators makes it vulnerable if surrounded. With limited speed and a small brain, it relies more on instinct and defence than strategy, making it vulnerable if caught off guard or isolated from its herd.

TIPS AND TACTICS
Teamwork is Best

You need to be quick and smart.

First, stay clear of its powerful spikes even from the sides. Keep moving swiftly to avoid getting caught and never fight it alone – working together is the key. Stay on the move and confuse it with quick changes in direction.

How to fight an...
ALTIRHINUS

KILLER FACT

It can swing its powerful neck and use its strong jaws to snap attackers.

STATS

HEIGHT	3 M
WEIGHT	1100 KG
LENGTH	7 M
KILLER RATING	3/10
INTELLIGENCE	4/10

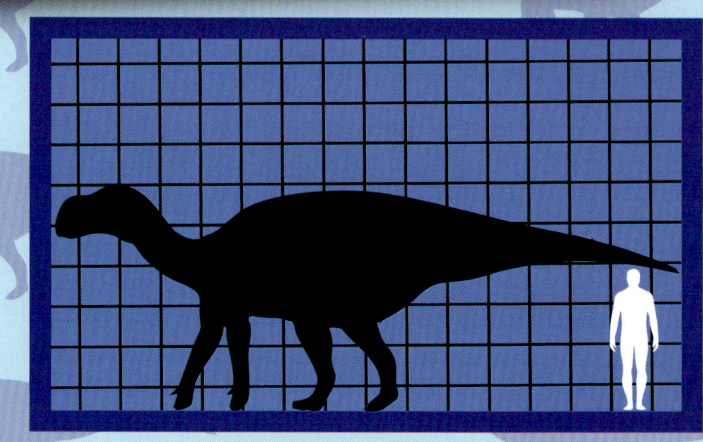

STRENGTH
Power and Protection

The Altirhinus relies on its size and strength to defend itself. With its long, robust jaws, it can deliver powerful bites. Its thick, heavy skull offers some protection and its large body makes it a challenge to take down.

WEAKNESS
Safety in Numbers

It doesn't have sharp claws or spikes for defence and it's also not the fastest. So without the advantage of speed or weapons, the Altirhinus relies heavily on its herd for safety, making it easier for predators to target it if it's isolated or caught off guard.

TIPS AND TACTICS
Quick Thinking

Use its love of vegetation to draw it away from its herd; tackling it solo will give you an advantage. By improving your ability to think quickly, you'll be ready to outsmart this giant plant-eater! Train your survival skills with practice challenges that force you to react fast, like switching direction at the last second or making decisions when under pressure. The more you practise, the sharper your instincts will become.

How to fight a...
HYPSILOPHODON

KILLER FACT

It has a row of razor-sharp spines running down its neck and back, ready to defend itself.

STATS

HEIGHT	I M
WEIGHT	40 KG
LENGTH	2 M
KILLER RATING	2/IO
INTELLIGENCE	5/IO

STRENGTH
Fast Feet, Fast Escape

Its lightweight body allows it to run at speeds up to 22 km/h, helping it escape danger. Its quick reflexes and sharp senses help it stay one step ahead in the wild, avoiding danger with swift, precise movements.

WEAKNESS
No Defences

The Hypsilophodon's small size and lack of powerful defences make it vulnerable.

Without sharp claws or a strong bite, it has no way to fight back against larger predators.

TIPS AND TACTICS
Speed Skills

To train to be a fast runner and catch a Hypsilophodon, focus on practising sprint intervals. Run short distances at full speed to build explosive power. Strengthen your legs with lunges and squats, while improving endurance by jogging longer distances. Pay attention to running form – keep your body upright, pump your arms, and push off with your toes to maximise speed.

How to fight an...
AMARGASAURUS

KILLER FACT

It is a real-life dragon with giant, spiky sails running down its neck!

STATS

HEIGHT	2.5 M
WEIGHT	9000 KG
LENGTH	12 M
KILLER RATING	4/10
INTELLIGENCE	4/10

STRENGTH
Spined Behemoth

The Amargasaurus is a fierce fighter, standing tall with its rows of spiky sails running down its back. When danger threatens, this plant-eater uses its sharp, pointed spines like a shield to scare off enemies.

WEAKNESS
Poor Balance

A weakness of the Amargasaurus lies in its reliance on its long neck for balance. If a predator can trip it or force it to stumble, this towering herbivore could have a tough time recovering.

TIPS AND TACTICS
The Spiked Menace

Stay low and fast, avoiding its sharp spines.

Its sides and legs are less protected, making them better targets than its killer back. Confusing it by circling quickly or attacking from different directions can throw it off. If you can unbalance it by tripping it or forcing it onto uneven ground, its long neck might work against it, leaving it vulnerable.

How to fight a...
CORYTHOSAURUS

KILLER FACT

It can blast out deep, eerie calls through its hollow crest – so loud they might shake the ground!

STATS

HEIGHT	3 M
WEIGHT	3000 KG
LENGTH	9 M
KILLER RATING	1/10
INTELLIGENCE	7/10

STRENGTH
Brains and Brawn

With legs designed for explosive leaps and a tail that swings like a battering ram, it's an elephant-sized acrobat with the agility of a deer. Its crown-like crest is not just as a striking visual feature but a tool for communication and intimidation in the wild.

WEAKNESS
Vulnerable Calls

Its biggest weakness is its reliance on sound for communication and coordination. Its distinctive crest, while perfect for trumpeting calls to its herd, becomes a liability when under attack. A well-aimed blow to the crest can disrupt its ability to signal for help.

TIPS AND TACTICS
Mastering Teamwork

Learn from the dinosaur itself by practising communication tactics with your friends.

Create clear, distinct calls for actions like "attack", "retreat", and "flank", and respond quickly to each one. This will help you mimic the fast, coordinated teamwork the Corythosaurus uses to stay ahead of predators.

How to fight an...
ARCHAEOCERATOPS

KILLER FACT

This lightning-fast herbivore dashes and weaves through danger to outpace hungry predators!

STATS

HEIGHT	0.5 M
WEIGHT	10 KG
LENGTH	1.3 M
KILLER RATING	1/10
INTELLIGENCE	4/10

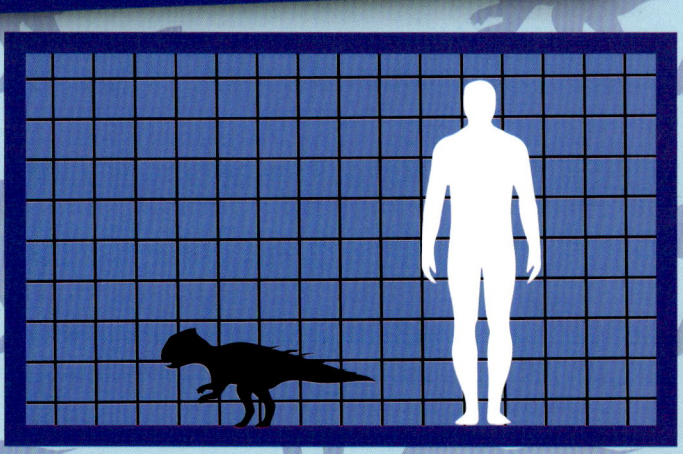

STRENGTH
Speed and Strategy

The Archaeoceratops uses its speed and nimbleness to outmanoeuvre larger predators, darting between obstacles to evade capture. Its small, sharp horns and frill act as a warning to those who get too close. Its real edge lies in its ability to stay low and fast.

WEAKNESS
Exhaustion Exposed

Its small size and limited stamina make prolonged escapes difficult. Once exhausted, it becomes slower and more vulnerable, unable to keep up its rapid manoeuvres or evade predators. The Archaeoceratops is easily cornered when its energy runs out.

TIPS AND TACTICS
Escape Game

Prepare with a "Speed and Escape" game! Set up an obstacle course with tunnels and tight spaces. One person is the predator, and the rest are Archaeoceratops trying to escape. You can only make quick bursts of speed for 2 seconds – no long sprints!

Avoid getting tagged while practising agility and clever manoeuvres to outwit the predator.

How to fight an...
ANKYLOSAURUS

KILLER FACT

The Ankylosaurus' armour is so tough that a T. rex's bite would struggle to break through it!

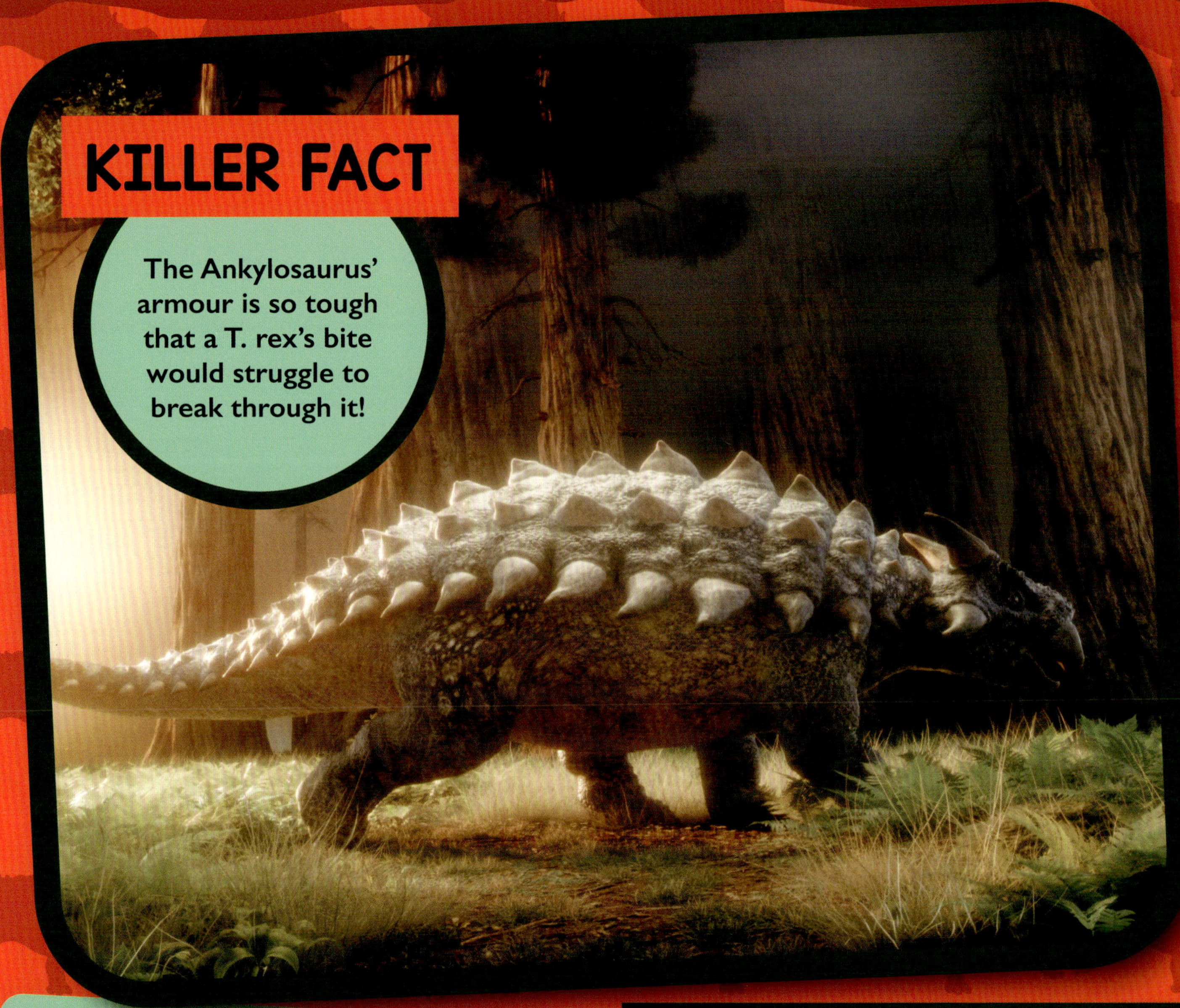

STATS

HEIGHT	1.5 M
WEIGHT	8000 KG
LENGTH	8 M
KILLER RATING	7/10
INTELLIGENCE	5/10

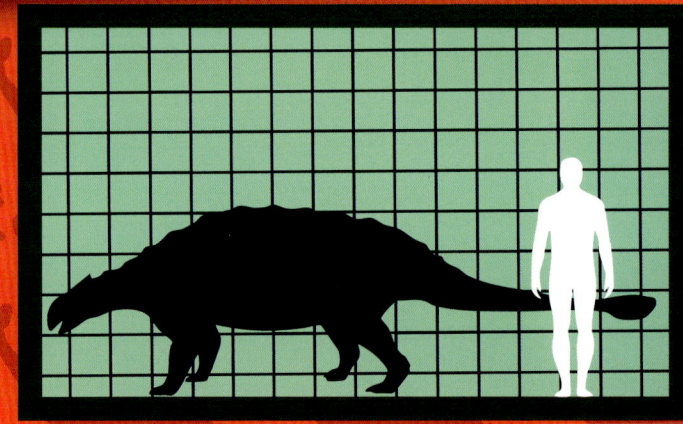

STRENGTH
Armoured Tank

It is like a real-life armoured tank that can camouflage itself into its surroundings. It is covered in tough, bony plates that protect it. Plus, it has a clubbed tail that's like a giant hammer. If a predator tries to attack, the Ankylosaurus can deliver a bone-crushing blow.

WEAKNESS
Slow and Steady

The Ankylosaurus is strong, but it has some weaknesses. Because of its heavy armour and short legs, it can only move at a slow pace. It can't run fast enough to escape danger. If it's caught off guard, it might struggle to get away before being hurt.

TIPS AND TACTICS
Be Patient & Observant!

It's all about patience and observation. By staying still and blending into its surroundings, the Ankylosaurus can watch for danger without being noticed. It waits for the right moment to attack with its clubbed tail.

Follow the Ankylosaurus' lead – be patient, stay observant and strike only when necessary.

How to fight an...
ARGENTINOSAURUS

KILLER FACT

Its footsteps are so heavy they cause small tremors, like an earthquake with every step!

STATS

HEIGHT	20 M
WEIGHT	70000 KG
LENGTH	35 M
KILLER RATING	3/10
INTELLIGENCE	3/10

STRENGTH
Power in Battle

In a fight, the Argentinosaurus uses its massive size to stay safe. Weighing as much as 12 adult elephants, it can crush predators by simply stepping on them! While it doesn't fight with claws or teeth, its sheer bulk makes it nearly impossible to take down.

WEAKNESS
Big and Clumsy

In open spaces, the Argentinosaurus relies on its long stride to move freely, but in thick jungles or rocky landscapes, its bulk makes it harder to move.

TIPS AND TACTICS
Move Like a Giant

To train for a fight with the Argentinosaurus, race along narrow tracks or weave between cones, pushing your balance and control to the limit.

To build strength, try fun exercises like jumping jacks and frog jumps. These will help you develop the muscle power needed for those big moves that make an impact in any battle.

How to fight a...
SUCHOMIMUS

KILLER FACT

Its snout is perfect for catching fish, giving it a unique edge as a swift, aquatic hunter!

STATS

HEIGHT	3.5 M
WEIGHT	6000 KG
LENGTH	11 M
KILLER RATING	9/10
INTELLIGENCE	4/10

STRENGTH
Precision in Combat

Its crocodile-like snout, filled with sharp teeth, is perfect for delivering quick, precise bites, especially when catching smaller prey or defending itself. It can use its claws to rake at enemies in close combat and maintain distance with its long, muscular legs.

WEAKNESS
Vulnerability in Battle

Its long, slender body, while ideal for fast movements, makes it less durable in a direct confrontation with larger, stronger predators. If it's unable to dodge attacks and is caught in a tight spot, its relatively fragile build could become a disadvantage.

TIPS AND TACTICS
Predator Chase

Play a game of "Predator Chase" with a ball to train like a Suchomimus.

One person is the "predator", and the others are Suchomimus, dodging obstacles and trying to grab the ball. The predator tries to tag them and keep hold of the ball. This builds speed, agility and quick reflexes — key traits for success in a fight!

How to fight a...

RAJASAURUS

KILLER FACT

The Rajasaurus boasts a striking crown of sweeping horns and a powerful build.

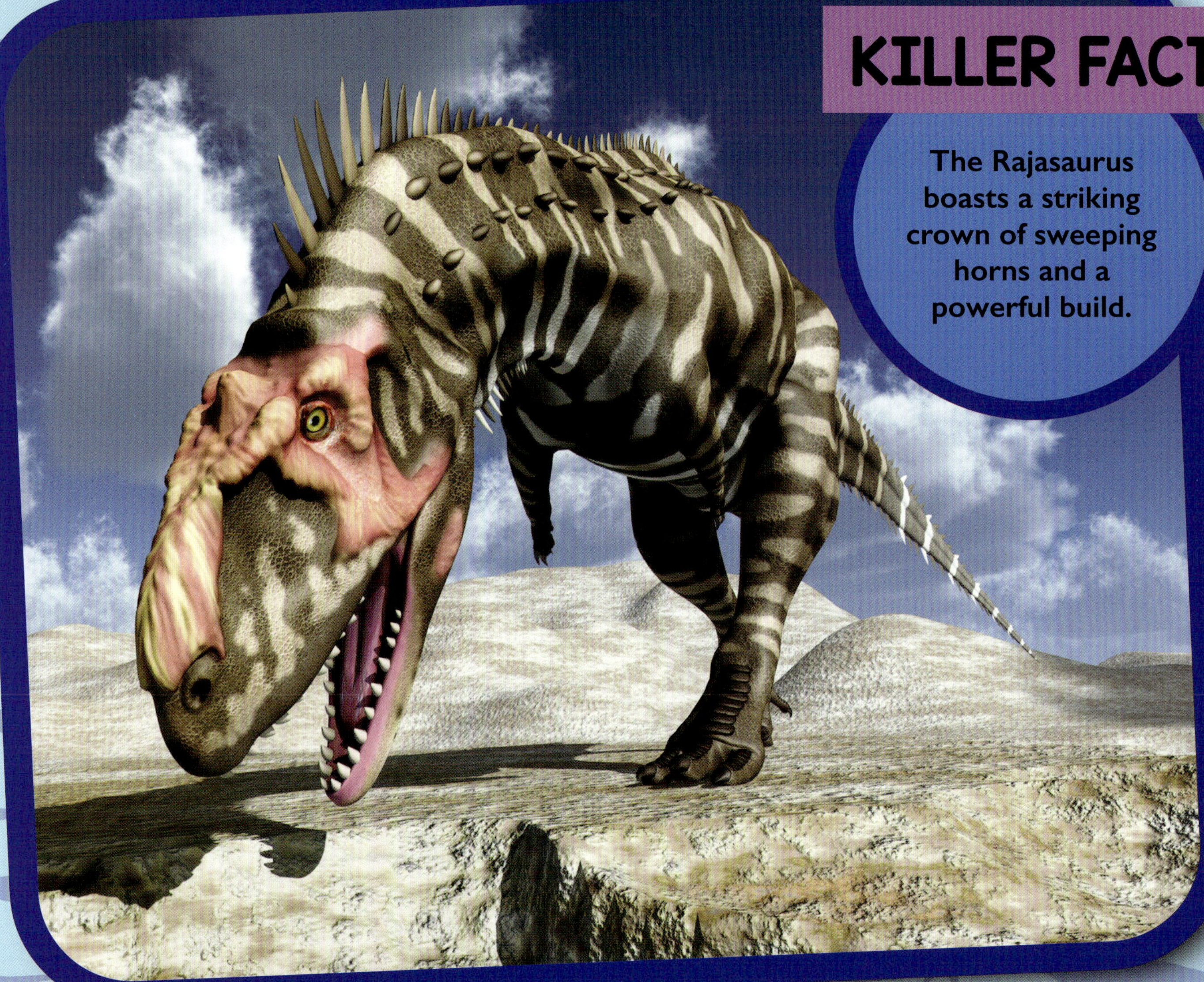

STATS

HEIGHT	3 M
WEIGHT	4000 KG
LENGTH	6.6 M
KILLER RATING	8/10
INTELLIGENCE	5/10

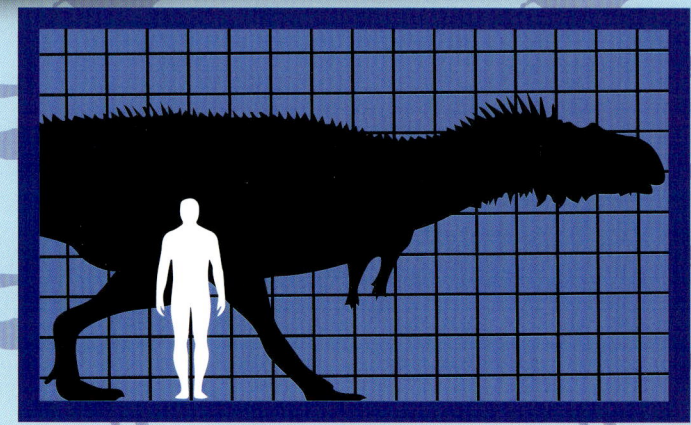

STRENGTH
Speed and Strike

In a fight, the Rajasaurus is like a speedy race car, darting around with sharp claws and a powerful bite. It's fast and uses its agility to dodge attacks, relying on quick strikes and sharp turns to overcome bigger foes. Speed and precision are its keys to victory.

WEAKNESS
Not a Heavy Hitter

The Rajasaurus' weakness is its smaller size and lighter build. While fast, it can't match larger, stronger predators like Tyrannosaurus or Giganotosaurus in a direct fight. If it's cornered or overpowered, its speed won't be enough to escape.

TIPS AND TACTICS
Dino Dodge

Focus on building your own agility and speed with specific drills. Set up a series of cones or markers in a zigzag pattern, then practise sprinting from one cone to the next, making sharp turns as you go. The goal is to improve your ability to change direction quickly. Incorporate quick starts and sudden stops to mimic the bursts of speed needed to fight the Rajasaurus.

How to fight an...
OMEISAURUS

KILLER FACT

The Omeisaurus' neck is about as long as two kayaks placed end to end.

STATS

HEIGHT	10 M
WEIGHT	10000 KG
LENGTH	20 M
KILLER RATING	2/10
INTELLIGENCE	3/10

STRENGTH
Towering Titan

The Omeisaurus towers over most predators like a living skyscraper! Its long, whip-like tail can deliver powerful swings, acting like a built-in defence system. With its enormous weight it can crush anything that gets too close.

WEAKNESS
No Agility

While its long neck helps it reach food, it also leaves its head vulnerable to attacks. Its massive body makes it difficult to move quickly. And if a predator manages to avoid its swinging tail, the Omeisaurus struggles to defend its smaller, less-protected areas.

TIPS AND TACTICS
Walk Tall

To get into the mind of an Omeisaurus, use buckets, tin cans or stilts to simulate its height. Use toys or cushions as "predators" and work on dodging or stepping over them without knocking them down. For tail defence, tie a long scarf or a skipping rope to your waist and swing it around to push the "predators" back. The goal is to experience what it's like to be big and mighty while staying balanced and vigilant.

How to fight a...
MONONYKUS

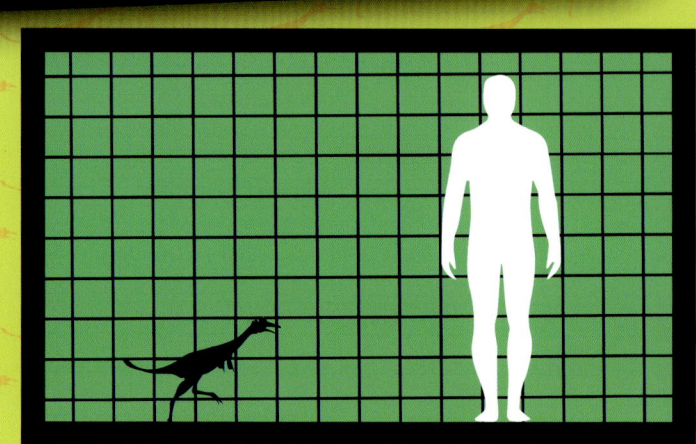

KILLER FACT

The single large claw on each of its hands is likely used to pry open insect nests!

STATS

HEIGHT	0.5 M
WEIGHT	3.5 KG
LENGTH	1.2 M
KILLER RATING	1/10
INTELLIGENCE	3/10

STRENGTH
Rapid Warrior

The Mononykus is a blur of speed and agility, dashing around with lightning-fast moves to avoid bigger predators. With its long legs and light frame, it can run at speeds of up to 40 km/h, leaving enemies struggling to catch up.

WEAKNESS
No Match for Giants

The Mononykus' single claw is good for quick slashes or digging, but it's not enough to fend off larger predators. If it gets caught or cornered, its small size and lack of natural armour make it vulnerable. If it can't escape quickly, it's in serious trouble.

TIPS AND TACTICS
Focus and Dash

Practise focusing your mind and sharpening your speed and agility. Try a "Dino Focus Drill" where you stand still for a few seconds with your eyes closed, take a deep breath, and then sprint to a target as quickly as possible once you open your eyes. The key is to block out distractions and concentrate solely on your goal, just like a Mononykus would when quickly darting away from predators or pursuing prey.

How to fight a...
NANOTYRANNUS

KILLER FACT

It may be a tiny tyrant, but its speed, agility and sharp mind make it a deadly predator!

STATS

HEIGHT	2 M
WEIGHT	1500 KG
LENGTH	5.5 M
KILLER RATING	8/10
INTELLIGENCE	7/10

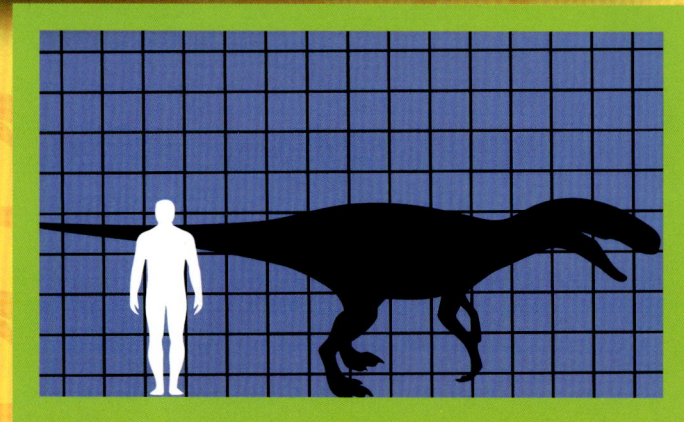

STRENGTH
Slick Slayer

This "tiny tyrant" is a lightning-fast predator with sharp teeth, strong legs and killer reflexes, making it a fierce opponent! Palaeontologists think the Nanotyrannus is just a juvenile T. rex, not a separate species. Either way, it's an incredible predator!

WEAKNESS
Bite Force

A unique weakness for Nanotyrannus in a fight could be its relatively thin jaws compared to a T. rex. While great for quick, slashing bites, its bite force may not be strong enough to take on heavily armoured prey or withstand prolonged combat with larger predators.

TIPS AND TACTICS
Close Combat

Use your size and strength to your advantage by forcing it into close combat, where its speed and agility are less effective. Stay alert for potential ambushes, especially if it's hunting in a pack, and position yourself defensively. Focus on targeting its weaker jaws, as they can't deliver the same powerful bite as larger predators.

How to fight a...
GIGANTSPINOSAURUS

KILLER FACT

It sports massive shoulder spines, making it a tough target for predators!

STATS

HEIGHT	2 M
WEIGHT	700 KG
LENGTH	4.2 M
KILLER RATING	3/10
INTELLIGENCE	2/10

STRENGTH
Shoulder Spikes

In battle, its shoulder spines serve as a formidable defence, capable of deterring predators with their sharp, rigid structure. These spines provide physical protection but may also be used for display, making the dinosaur look even more intimidating.

WEAKNESS
Weak Bite

A weakness for the Gigantspinosaurus in a fight is its small head and weak bite. With a relatively small mouth and teeth adapted for plant-eating, it struggles to inflict significant damage on predators or opponents, since it relies more on defence.

TIPS AND TACTICS
Head Attack

Aim for its head and vulnerable underbelly, where its armour is less protective.

Keep your distance, striking from the sides or behind, as it struggles with mobility.

Using agility to dodge its defensive swipes could also give you the upper hand.

How to fight a...
DEINONYCHUS

KILLER FACT

This kind of dinosaur hunts cooperatively, like modern-day wolves!

STATS

HEIGHT	1.5 M
WEIGHT	100 KG
LENGTH	3.4 M
KILLER RATING	8/10
INTELLIGENCE	9/10

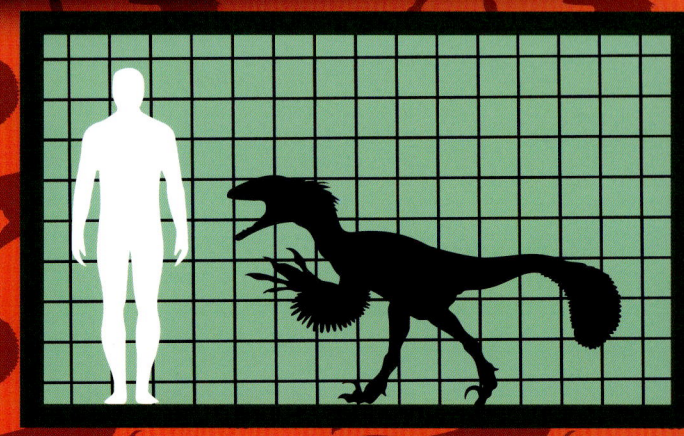

STRENGTH
Killer Claw

One of Deinonychus' key strengths in a fight is its retractable sickle claw on each foot, which it uses to slash at its opponent, leaving deep, crippling wounds. This claw, combined with its speed and agility, allows it to strike quickly and decisively.

WEAKNESS
Where's the Defence?

A key weakness for Deinonychus in a fight is its limited defence; unlike other theropods with tougher hides or armour, its lightweight body and lack of significant protection make it vulnerable to attacks. This leaves it relying solely on speed and agility.

TIPS AND TACTICS
Watch Out!

It will try to strike with its sickle claw.

Keep your distance to avoid close combat, where its speed and claws are most dangerous. If possible, use brute strength to overpower it, as Deinonychus struggles against larger, stronger foes. Watch for its quick attacks and try to tire it out by maintaining control of the battle's pace.

How to fight an...
APATOSAURUS

KILLER FACT

It has a tail so strong it can easily knock over a tree!

STATS

HEIGHT	9 M
WEIGHT	41000 KG
LENGTH	23 M
KILLER RATING	2/10
INTELLIGENCE	1/10

STRENGTH
Jurassic Giant

Watch out for the Apatosaurus' massive tail, which can swing like a giant wrecking ball, hitting with the force of a huge sledgehammer slamming into a wall. Imagine that power! Plus, its giant size makes it very tricky for any predator to take down.

WEAKNESS
Weak Spot

A unique weakness of Apatosaurus in a fight is that its teeth aren't cut out for battle. While it can eat plants easily, its teeth are small and flat, perfect for grinding leaves, but not suited for defending itself or fighting back against predators.

TIPS AND TACTICS
Be Ready for Battle

To avoid the swinging tail, trap the Apatosaurus using the terrain. Find a narrow area like a canyon or between large rocks where it struggles to turn.

Create distractions, like loud noises or moving objects, to lure it in. Once it's close, block its escape routes with boulders or fallen trees. The Apatosaurus will be trapped, unable to pivot or charge effectively in the confined space.

How to fight a...
MIRAGAIA

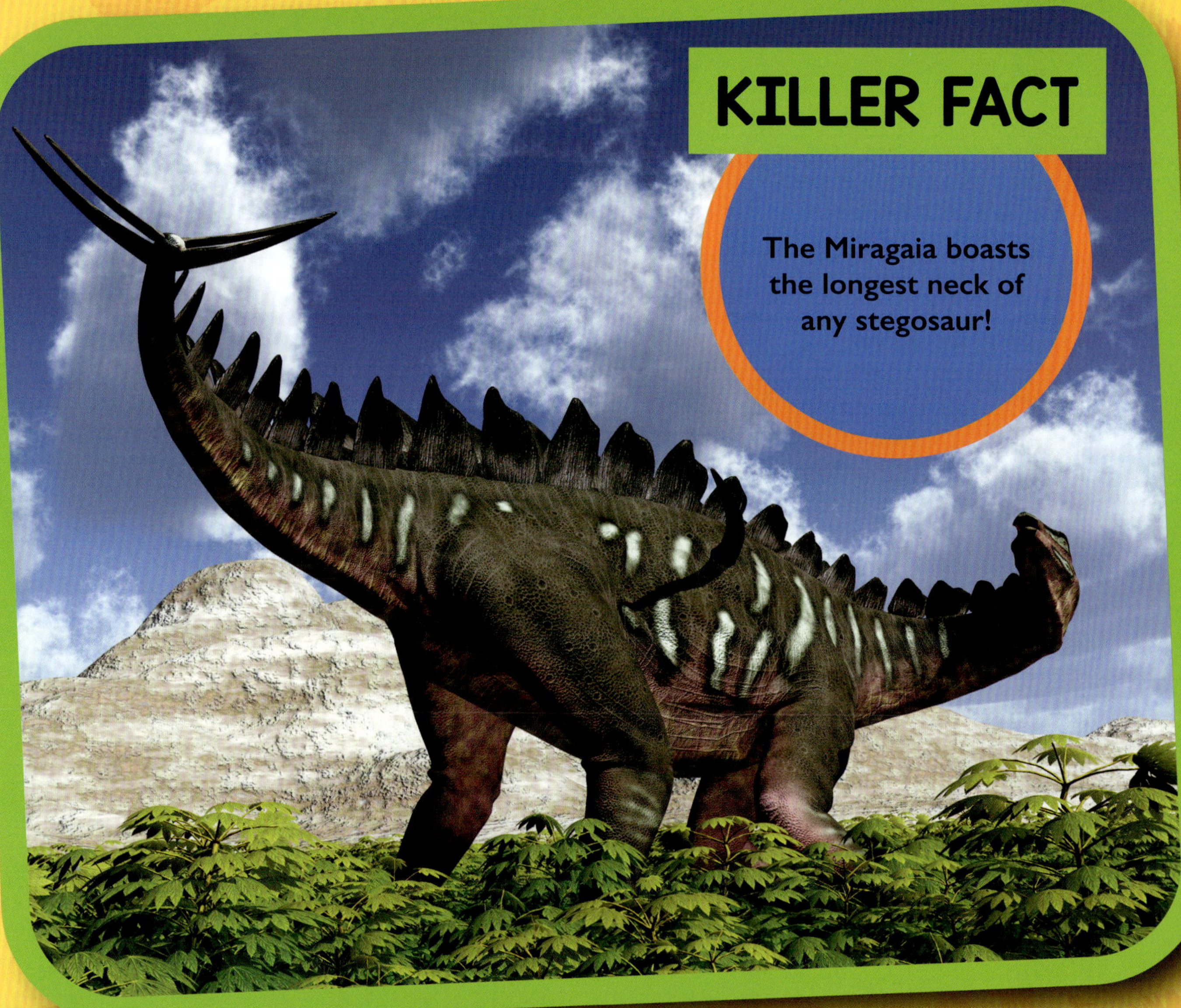

KILLER FACT

The Miragaia boasts the longest neck of any stegosaur!

STATS

HEIGHT	2.5 M
WEIGHT	2000 KG
LENGTH	6.5 M
KILLER RATING	2/10
INTELLIGENCE	1/10

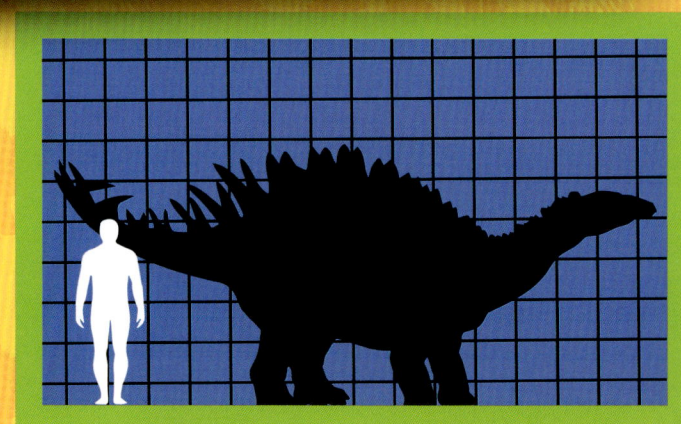

STRENGTH
Neck Strikes

In a battle, the Miragaia uses its super-long neck, which it can twist and swing like a giant lashing rope, keeping predators at bay. Its tail is also like a giant broom swinging through the air. It can swat predators away with the force of a huge gust of wind.

WEAKNESS
Slow and Stiff

With its massive, heavy body, the Miragaia moves as if it's carrying a giant tree on its back – slow and cumbersome! If a fast predator starts darting around, escaping or dodging might be a real challenge for this giant herbivore.

TIPS AND TACTICS
Dodge the Dino Tail

Try playing "Stego Stalk"! One player is the Miragaia and stands in the centre slowly turning in place. The other players must sneak up and tap them without being seen moving. If the "Miragaia" spots someone moving, they have to go back to the start. This helps with stealth, patience and quick reflexes: perfect for practising how to approach a real Miragaia without getting whacked by its tail!

How to fight a...
CRYOLOPHOSAURUS

KILLER FACT

It sports a distinctive crest on its head, which makes it look like a dinosaur rockstar!

STATS

HEIGHT 3 M
WEIGHT 500 KG
LENGTH 8 M
KILLER RATING 7/10
INTELLIGENCE 7/10

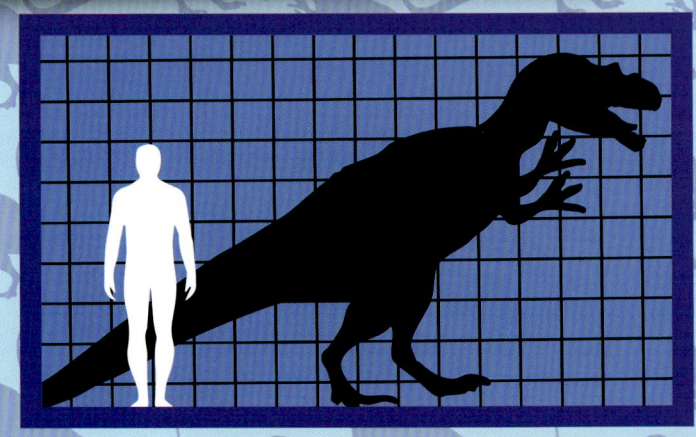

STRENGTH
Swift Striker

With its lightweight build and long legs, it can likely run at speeds of up to 48 km/h. This speed, combined with sharp claws and powerful jaws, means it can dart in and deliver quick, decisive attacks before its opponent even has time to react!

WEAKNESS
Crest Downfall

Its weakness is its exposed crest on its head.

While it may be used for display or communication, it's also a vulnerable spot that predators could target. If a larger opponent manages to land a blow to it, they could cause significant damage.

TIPS AND TACTICS
Feathers of Fear

Craft a headdress with bright feathers, twigs and leaves. Add some vibrant colours and textured materials to make it stand out, and wear it like a true prehistoric warrior.

With this headdress on, you'll look even scarier than the Cryolophosaurus, tricking it into thinking you're a tough competitor or a powerful ally.

How to fight an...
ARIZONASAURUS

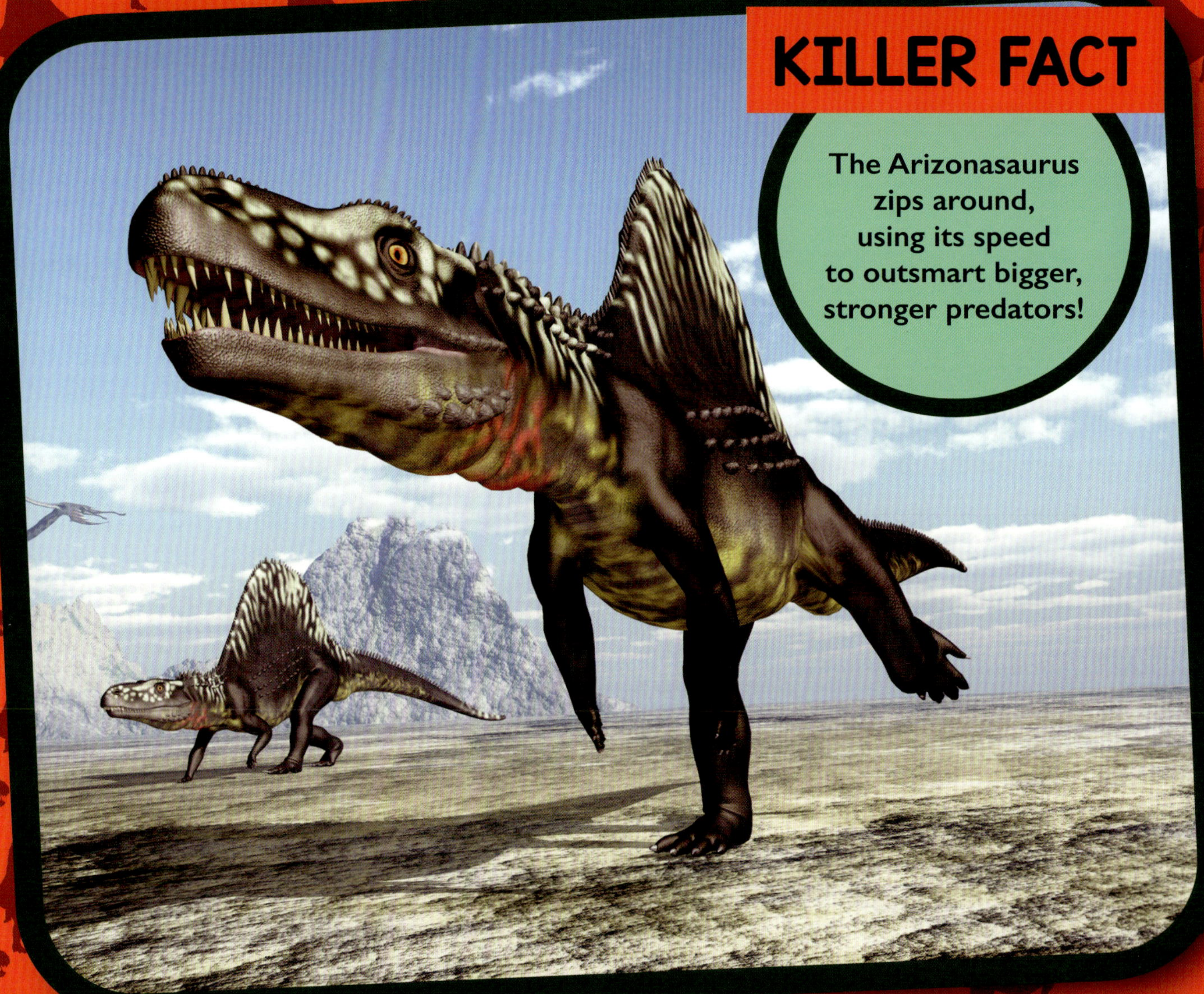

KILLER FACT

The Arizonasaurus zips around, using its speed to outsmart bigger, stronger predators!

STATS

HEIGHT	1 M
WEIGHT	227 KG
LENGTH	3 M
KILLER RATING	4/10
INTELLIGENCE	4/10

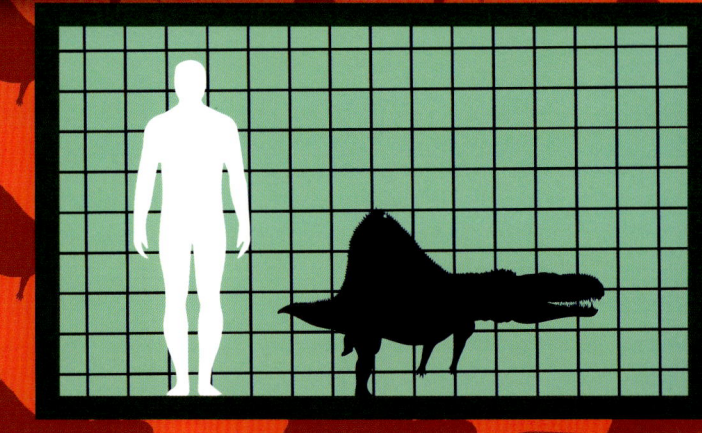

The Arizonasaurus is not technically a dinosaur, but a sail-backed reptile from the archosaur family.

STRENGTH
Rapid Sailor

The Arizonasaurus' sail is its secret weapon!

Like a giant, flashy flag on its back – the sail makes it seem bigger and more intimidating. It might also use the sail to sway back and forth, making it harder for enemies to get a good shot in.

WEAKNESS
Speed Can't Save It

While Arizonasaurus can zoom around fast, it isn't built for heavy-duty battles like some of the larger, more powerful dinosaurs. Its body is designed for agility, allowing it to dodge and dart away from danger, rather than stand toe-to-toe and fight.

TIPS AND TACTICS
Strategies for the Win

Since it's more agile than strong, your best bet is to stay one step ahead – set traps, throw distractions, or use the environment to your advantage. That flashy sail on its back might look impressive, but it's a big target you can use to throw it off balance. Keep your distance and use clever tricks to wear it down without getting too close.

How to fight a...
GIGANTORAPTOR

KILLER FACT

Its huge eyes help it spot prey from a distance, making it an excellent lookout.

STATS

HEIGHT	5 M
WEIGHT	2000 KG
LENGTH	8 M
KILLER RATING	4/10
INTELLIGENCE	8/10

STRENGTH
Lightning-Fast Giant

Despite being massive, it's surprisingly nimble and able to tear around opponents while inflicting swift, powerful kicks with its long legs. Its feathered body helps with balance, making it agile enough to deliver quick slashes with its claws and peck with its beak.

WEAKNESS
Fragile Legs

While it's fast and agile, it's not built for direct combat, relying more on dodging than overpowering its opponent. Its long, slender legs, though great for speed, are in danger of being targeted in a fight, especially by stronger attackers.

TIPS AND TACTICS
Aim Low

Its enormous size gives it power, while its long, muscular legs are crucial for speed and stability. If you can get close enough, aim for its legs to slow it down and reduce its mobility. Striking its knees or tendons could cause it to stumble or lose its balance, making it harder for the Gigantoraptor to chase or strike effectively. But don't rush in unless you're sure you can land a decisive blow!

How to fight a...
PACHYCEPHALOSAURUS

KILLER FACT

Its skull is about 25 cm thick in some places – perfect for use as a bony battering ram!

STATS

HEIGHT	2 M
WEIGHT	450 KG
LENGTH	4.5 M
KILLER RATING	2/10
INTELLIGENCE	5/10

STRENGTH
Headbutt Hero

The Pachycephalosaurus relies on its unique thick, domed skull as its main strength. It can deliver powerful headbutts, similar to modern animals like rams, using its skull to knock back rivals and defend itself from predators.

WEAKNESS
Fast Food

Larger carnivores might see the Pachycephalosaurus as a tasty snack, with its low-fat body and not much to protect it – aside from its tough skull! It's the perfect "fast food" for hungry predators, especially if it's all alone and caught off guard!

TIPS AND TACTICS
Defeating the Dino

Keep your distance to avoid its powerful headbutts and use speed to outmanoeuvre it since it's not the fastest.

Target its vulnerable body, especially the legs and sides, where it's less protected. After it strikes with a headbutt, use the moment when it's off balance to strike back quickly before it can recover.

How to fight a...
DAKOSAURUS

KILLER FACT

Its crocodile-like jaws are so strong they can snap shut with the force of a steel trap!

STATS

HEIGHT	1 M
WEIGHT	700 KG
LENGTH	5 M
KILLER RATING	7/10
INTELLIGENCE	7/10

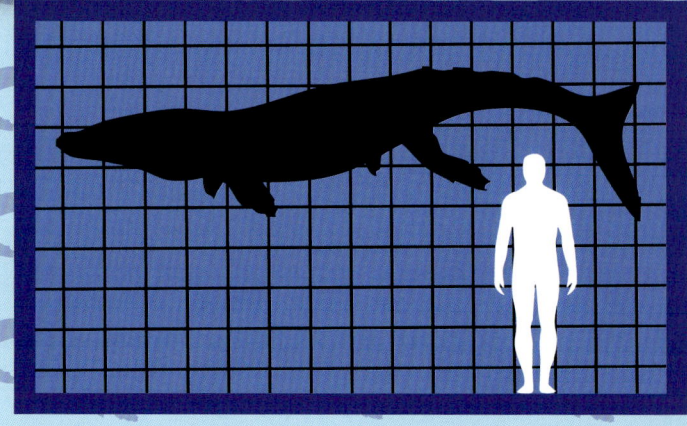

Dakosaurus is a marine reptile related to crocodiles, so it's not technically a dinosaur.

STRENGTH
Deadly Ocean Predator

The Dakosaurus uses its powerful jaws and sharp teeth to quickly capture and tear into prey. Its streamlined body and strong tail make it an agile swimmer, allowing it to outmanoeuvre opponents and strike with precision.

WEAKNESS
Struggles on Land

The Dakosaurus' main weakness in a fight is its vulnerability on land. While it's a fearsome predator in the water, it struggles if forced onto land or in shallow water where it can't fully utilise its swimming agility.

TIPS AND TACTICS
Keep Your Distance

Avoid the water where it's most powerful and focus on keeping your distance. If you get close, aim for its weaker spots, like the underbelly or eyes, and use the environment to limit its movement.

Stay defensive and dodge its powerful bite, waiting for the perfect moment to strike back.

Learning about dinosaurs is like piecing together a giant puzzle from millions of years ago! Scientists, called palaeontologists, study fossils – ancient bones, teeth and footprints left behind by dinosaurs. They carefully dig up and examine these fossils, trying to figure out how dinosaurs lived, what they looked like, and how they behaved.

But, here's the thing: we don't have actual photographs of dinosaurs! Instead, artists use the clues from fossils to create amazing, but imperfect, pictures of what dinosaurs might have looked like.

The pictures in this book are based on the best research, but they are still interpretations, meaning no two artists are likely to show a dinosaur exactly the same way!

And the best part? Dinosaurs are still being discovered today! Every year, palaeontologists find new fossils in places all over the world. These discoveries help scientists update what we know about dinosaurs. Sometimes new fossils change everything we thought we knew, like revealing a new species or showing that dinosaurs had feathers or colourful skin. It's like opening a mystery box of new clues, and each discovery helps us get closer to the truth about these incredible creatures.

So, while images of dinosaurs might not be 100% exact, they are based on the coolest science we have today. Who knows? Maybe one day you'll help discover a new dinosaur and become part of the adventure of learning more about these amazing creatures that once ruled the Earth! The world of dinosaurs is still full of surprises and new research is always changing the way we see the past!

You've reached the end of this guide to fighting and defeating dinosaurs. Along the way, you've learned about their strengths, weaknesses and how they lived millions of years ago. Just like the dinosaurs, you have unique strengths – whether it's your agility, intelligence or resilience.

By understanding and embracing your own abilities, you can build confidence to face any challenge that comes your way. Just as the dinosaurs used their special traits to survive, you can tap into your skills to navigate the obstacles in your life, overcome fears and tackle tough situations with the same determination and creativity they did millions of years ago!

Activity Ideas

Draw your favourite dinosaur and describe why you think it's the coolest.

Design some dino-protective armour. Think about what you'd need to stay safe – sharp spikes, a tough shell, or even camouflage.

List your super strengths and how you use them to overcome challenges just like a dinosaur would.

Create a hybrid dinosaur. Mix two or more dinosaurs together and give your new creature a brilliant name.

Write a battle plan for how you'd outsmart a T. rex using only your brainpower and what's in your backpack.

Invent a Dino Survival Kit. Choose five essential items you'd take on a dinosaur adventure and explain why.

Make up your own dinosaur. What does it eat? How big is it? Does it have any secret powers?

Build a miniature dino battleground using toys, cardboard or modelling clay – and act out an epic scene.

Create a comic strip showing how you'd beat a dinosaur using a clever trick or trap.

Set up a "Dino Challenge Course" – an obstacle course inspired by how different dinosaurs might move, hunt or escape.

Write a dino fact-or-fiction quiz. Try to catch your friends out with some tricky questions.

Draw yourself as a dinosaur. What features would you have? A tail? Claws? Super-speed?

Write a "Dino Peace Treaty". How would you convince the dinosaurs to stop fighting and work together?

Design your perfect dinosaur hideout. Would it be in the trees? Underground? Camouflaged in a cave?

Write a diary entry from the point of view of a dinosaur who meets you: "Today I met a strange, brave creature…"

Create a dinosaur battle card game. Give each dinosaur strengths, weaknesses and special moves – then play against a friend.

Make a timeline of the dinosaur ages. Include when different species lived and draw little sketches to go with each one.

Write a short story about waking up in the time of dinosaurs – what would you do, where would you go, and how would you survive?

Invent a dinosaur-themed board game. Include things like lava pits, hidden fossils and surprise dinosaur attacks!

Design a flag or emblem for your dinosaur-fighting team – what symbols would show off your bravery or skills?

Host a "Dino Debate". Choose two dinosaurs and argue which one would win in a friendly battle – use facts and imagination!

Dinosaurs may be extinct, but they continue to inspire us to think big, get creative and explore the past. Keep asking questions and always stay curious!